# DINOSAURS, REPTILES, AND BIRDS

## How to Use Your SD-X Reader with This Book

This highly informative book introduces you and your child to dinosaurs, reptiles, and birds in a new interactive format. You can read the book and study the rich illustrations, but a touch of the SD-X Reader adds in-depth audefinitions, and learning games to the pictures and text.

1. Press the Power button to turn the SD-X Reader on or off. Th the SD-X Reader is on.

2. Touch the volume buttons found on this page or on the Table of Contents page in this book to adjust the volume.

3. Throughout the book, words in this color provide additional information when they're touched with the SD-X Reader. Objects on the page may play additional audio.

4. At the top left corner of each spread, you'll see circles like these: ●●
Touch a circle to start a learning game or quiz. Touch the same circle again to stop playing the game. Touch another circle to start another learning game or quiz.

5. Some learning games will ask you to use Ⓣ Ⓕ buttons or Ⓐ Ⓑ buttons to answer. For other learning games, touch objects on the page to answer.

6. When you've answered all the questions in a learning game, you'll hear your score.

7. After two minutes of inactivity, the SD-X Reader will beep and go to sleep.

8. If the batteries are low, the SD-X Reader will beep twice and the LED will start blinking. Replace the batteries by following the instructions on the next page. The SD-X Reader uses two AAA batteries.

9. To use headphones or earbuds, plug them into the headphone jack on the bottom of the SD-X Reader.

---

### CHANGE THE VOLUME WITH THESE BUTTONS:

**UP**   **DOWN**

**Battery Information**
Includes two replaceable AAA batteries (UM-4 or LR03).

**Battery Installation**
1. Open battery door with small screwdriver.
2. Install new batteries according to +/- polarity. If batteries are not installed properly, the device will not function.
3. Replace battery door; secure with small screw.

**Battery Safety**
Batteries must be replaced by adults only. Properly dispose of used batteries. See battery manufacturer for disposal recommendations. Do not mix alkaline, standard (carbon-zinc), or rechargeable (nickel-cadmium) batteries. Do not mix old and new batteries. Only recommended batteries of the same or equivalent type should be used. Remove weakened or dead batteries. Never short-circuit the supply terminals. Non-rechargeable batteries are not to be recharged. Do not use rechargeable batteries. If batteries are swallowed, in the USA, promptly see a doctor and have the doctor phone 1-202-625-3333 collect. In other countries, have the doctor call your local poison control center. This product uses 2 AAA batteries (2 X 1.5V = 3.0 V). Use batteries of the same or equivalent type as recommended. The supply terminals are not to be short-circuited. Batteries should be changed when sounds mix, distort, or become otherwise unintelligible as batteries weaken. The electrostatic discharge may interfere with the sound module. If this occurs, please simply restart the sound module by pressing any key.

In Europe, the dustbin symbol indicates that batteries, rechargeable batteries, button cells, battery packs, and similar materials must not be discarded in household waste. Batteries containing hazardous substances are harmful to the environment and to health. Please help to protect the environment from health risks by telling your children to dispose of batteries properly and by taking batteries to local collection points. Batteries handled in this manner are safely recycled.

**Warning:** Changes or modifications to this unit not expressly approved by the party responsible for compliance could void the user's authority to operate the equipment.

**NOTE:** This equipment has been tested and found to comply with the limits for a Class B digital device, pursuant to Part 15 of the FCC Rules. These limits are designed to provide reasonable protection against harmful interference in a residential installation. This equipment generates, uses, and can radiate radio frequency energy and, if not installed and used in accordance with the instructions, may cause harmful interference to radio communications. However, there is no guarantee that interference will not occur in a particular installation. If this equipment does cause harmful interference to radio or television reception, which can be determined by turning the equipment off and on, the user is encouraged to try to correct the interference by one or more of the following measures: Reorient or relocate the receiving antenna. Increase the separation between the equipment and receiver. Connect the equipment into an outlet on a circuit different from that to which the receiver is connected. Consult the dealer or an experienced radio TV technician for help.

Cover image sources: Art Explosion, Corbis, Image Bank, PhotoDisc

Product and sound element design, engineering, and reproduction are proprietary technologies of Publications International, Ltd.

Published by Louis Weber, C.E.O., Publications International, Ltd.
7373 North Cicero Avenue                    Ground Floor, 59 Gloucester Place
Lincolnwood, Illinois 60712                    London W1U 8JJ

Customer Service: 1-888-724-0144 or customer_service@pilbooks.com

**www.pilbooks.com**

 Publications International, Ltd.

Manufactured in China.

8 7 6 5 4 3 2 1

ISBN-10: 1-4508-0359-8
ISBN-13: 978-1-4508-0359-5

# CONTENTS

**CHANGE THE VOLUME WITH THESE BUTTONS:**

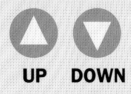

**UP   DOWN**

# Terrible Lizards

Dinosaurs dominated the Earth for 170 million years, from the late Triassic to the late Cretaceous periods, when the supercontinents of Laurasia and Gondwana were splitting into the landmasses of today. The mass *extinction* of the dinosaurs about 65 million years ago left *fossil* remains, including footprints, eggs, and bones. Finding these fossils has enabled scientists to learn about dinosaurs' posture, size, diet, and many other aspects of their lives. Prehistoric lizards included *herbivores* and *carnivores* of extraordinary size and striking shapes.

**Flexible Neck**
Moved more easily because the vertebrae were light in weight

## Lizard Legs

**①** LIZARDS

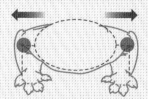

**②** CROCODILES

| DEINOS | SAURO |
|--------|-------|
| Terrible | Lizard |

**IDENTITY**

The term Dinosauria was proposed for these extinct reptiles by paleontologist Richard Owen in 1842. The name of each species is based on characteristics of its shape and physiology, the name of its discoverer, or the location where it was found.

*Barosaurus*
or "heavy reptile" ▶

**③** DINOSAURS

## From Primitive Forms

| Herrerasaurus<br>Length: 13 feet<br>(4 m) | Coelophysis<br>Length: 9.2 feet<br>(2.8 m) | Eoraptor<br>Length: 3 feet<br>(1 m) | Mussaurus<br>Length: 6.6 feet<br>(2 m) | Plateosaurus<br>Length: 26 feet<br>(8 m) | Dryosaurus<br>Length: 13 feet<br>(4 m) | Megalosaurus<br>Length: 29.5 feet<br>(9 m) | Brachiosaurus<br>Length: 82 feet<br>(25 m) |
|---|---|---|---|---|---|---|---|

| TRIASSIC PERIOD  251-199.6 MILLION YEARS AGO | JURASSIC PERIOD |
|---|---|

# 110 tons
## (100 metric tons)
### ESTIMATED WEIGHT OF
### AN *ARGENTINOSAURUS*

**SIR DINOSAUR**

# Over 2,000
### SPECIES OF DINOSAURS HAVE
### BEEN CATALOGED AT PRESENT.

## SAURISCHIANS
Pelvic structure of
saurischian dinosaurs

## FIERCE LIZARDS
**Tyrannosaurus rex,** a carnivore

## ORNITHISCHIANS
In spite of their name,
these animals are not
ancestors of today's birds.

## ORNITHISCHIANS
**Comptosaurus,** a herbivore

| *Stegosaurus* Length: 30 feet (9 m) | *Camarasaurus* Length: 66 feet (20 m) | *Therizinosaurus* Length: 39 feet (12 m) | *Caudipteryx* Length: 3 feet (1 m) | *Suchomimus* Length: 43 feet (13 m) | *Giganotosaurus* Length: 49 feet (15 m) | *Corythosaurus* Length: 33 feet (10 m) |
|---|---|---|---|---|---|---|

**199.6-145.5 MILLION YEARS AGO** | **CRETACEOUS PERIOD  145.5-65.5 MILLION YEARS AGO**

# The Triassic Period

In the earliest part of the period, the first representatives of today's *amphibians* appeared, and toward the end of the period the first *mammals* emerged. In the middle to late Triassic Period, the many families of ferns and conifers appeared that continue to exist today, as well as other groups of plants that are now extinct.

VEGETATION

**Flora** ▾

## Extinction

Dinosaurs spread rapidly as other groups of species died out.

## ▼ A New World

The supercontinent Pangea was the
home of dinosaurs and other animals.

# 250 to 203
## million years ago

The Earth had only one continental mass, called
Pangea. This continent had an upper region called
Laurasia and a lower region called Gondwana.

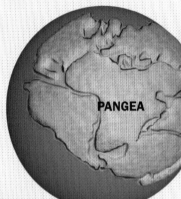

PANGEA

NUMEROUS
SPECIES

Fauna ►

# The "Age of Reptiles"

During the first period of the Mesozoic Era, the earliest crocodiles began to develop, along with turtles and frogs. The pterosaurs ruled the air and the ichthyosaurs the water. The dinosaurs appeared in the Middle Triassic, approximately 250 million years ago. Toward the end of the Triassic Period, many other reptiles declined dramatically, and the dinosaurs began their reign.

## The First Dinosaurs

Most early dinosaur *fossils* have been found in South America.

**Eoraptor** ▶

TAIL

SPINAL COLUMN

▲
*Coelophysis*

*Mussaurus* ▶

## HERRERASAURUS

| | |
|---|---|
| Size | 13 feet (4 m) |
| Diet | Carnivorous |
| Habitat | Conifer Forests |
| Epoch | Late Triassic |
| Range | South America |

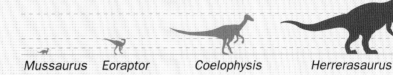

*Mussaurus*  *Eoraptor*  *Coelophysis*  *Herrerasaurus*

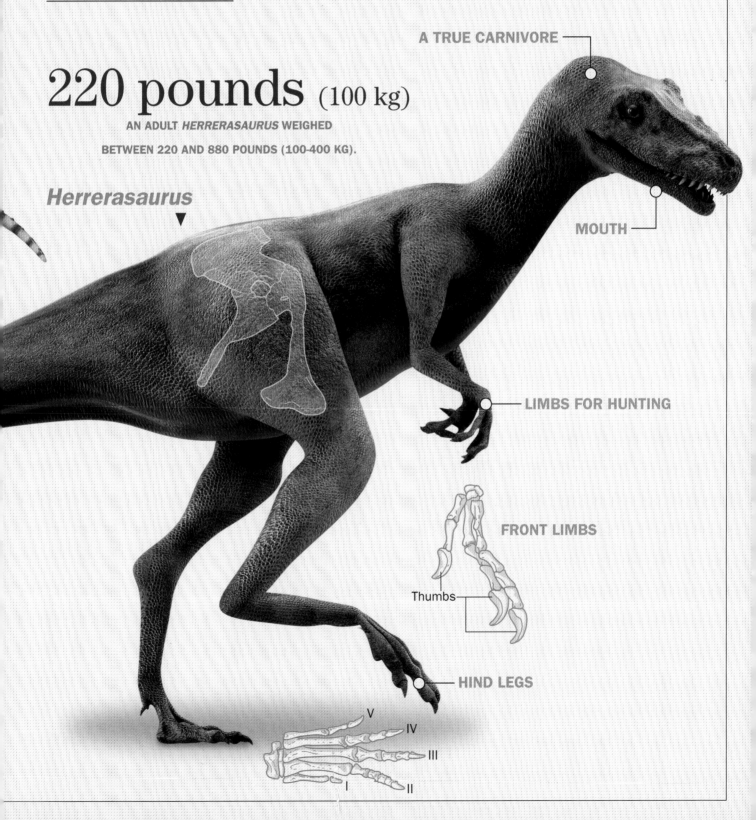

A TRUE CARNIVORE

# 220 pounds (100 kg)

AN ADULT *HERRERASAURUS* WEIGHED

BETWEEN 220 AND 880 POUNDS (100-400 KG).

## *Herrerasaurus*
▼

MOUTH

LIMBS FOR HUNTING

FRONT LIMBS

Thumbs

HIND LEGS

V
IV
III
I
II

# The First Giant Herbivore

This primitive saurischian was among the first to usher in the age of the dinosaurs in the late Triassic Period, about 210 million years ago. It was clearly one of the first that fed exclusively on plants and that reached the immense sizes typical of herbivores. Many fossils have been found in over 50 separate locations. The secret of this dinosaur's survival is believed to have been the lack of competition for food, since no other herbivore of the time grew as large.

*Plateosaurus* ▶
*engelhardti*

Movement

EVENTUAL BIPEDS

Head

In the
Treetops

## PLATEOSAURUS

| | |
|---|---|
| Size | 26-33 feet (8-10 m) |
| Diet | Herbivorous |
| Habitat | Semiarid Regions |
| Epoch | Late Triassic |
| Range | Europe |

WHERE
IT LIVED

AND
UAL
IMORPHISM

Females
were
dominant.

WEIGHT
BEARING
TOES

Upper Limb

Claw

## Defensive Claw

Hind
Foot

# The Jurassic Period

During this period, dinosaurs diversified greatly and spread out to occupy land, sea, and air. Along with large *herbivores*, there were salamanders, lizards, and the *Archaeopteryx*, the most ancient bird known. The climate of the Jurassic Period was mild, with moisture-laden winds from the ocean. They brought great downpours, enabling forests to cover wide areas of land.

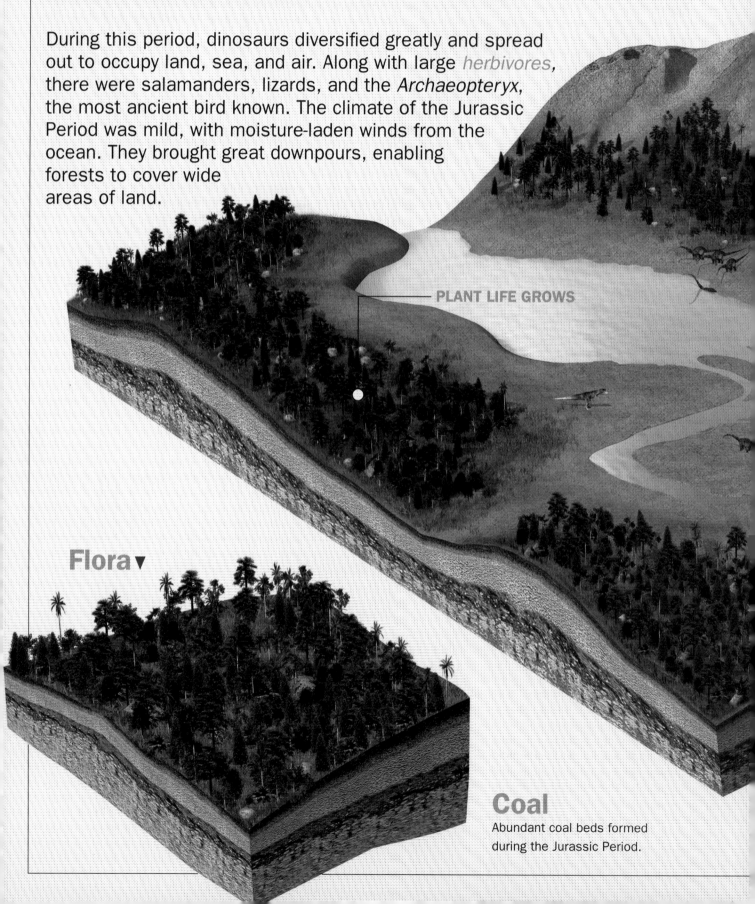

PLANT LIFE GROWS

**Flora** ▼

## Coal

Abundant coal beds formed during the Jurassic Period.

# The Green Planet

The climate was warm and temperate on most areas of the planet.

# 208 to 140
## million years ago

The Earth began to divide. During the Jurassic Period, North America drifted north and separated from what is now South America. North America formed part of Laurasia with what would become Europe. Antarctica, South America, India, and Australia formed Gondwana to the south.

**LAURASIA**

**GONDWANA**

ORNITHISCHIANS

**SHARED WORLD**
*Marsupials* and birds appeared.

Fauna ▶

# Different Species

The gradual splitting of Pangea created new ecological environments. The increased humidity enabled the growth of dense vegetation. This flourishing environment increased the number of dinosaur species. In contrast, these conditions forced a decline in the majority of synapsids, and the archosaurs—the group that includes crocodiles—largely disappeared. Other species also found their ecological niches and multiplied. These species included sea creatures, such as sharks and rays, that resemble their modern relatives, as well as ray-finned fish with sharp teeth, such as the fierce *predator* *Aspidorhynchus*.

## Giants of the Mesozoic

**Megalosaurus** ▶
means "large lizard"

▲
**Dryosaurus**
means "oak reptile"

**Camarasaurus**
means "chambered lizard"
◀

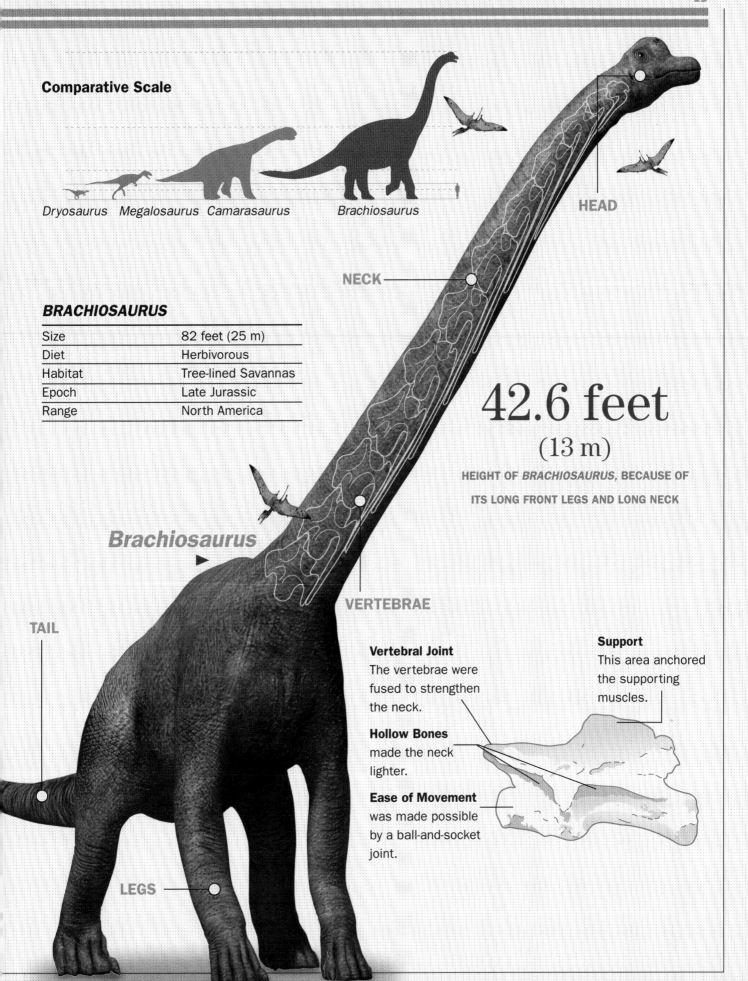

**Comparative Scale**

Dryosaurus   Megalosaurus   Camarasaurus   Brachiosaurus

HEAD

NECK

### BRACHIOSAURUS

| Size | 82 feet (25 m) |
|---|---|
| Diet | Herbivorous |
| Habitat | Tree-lined Savannas |
| Epoch | Late Jurassic |
| Range | North America |

# 42.6 feet
## (13 m)

HEIGHT OF *BRACHIOSAURUS*, BECAUSE OF
ITS LONG FRONT LEGS AND LONG NECK

*Brachiosaurus* ►

VERTEBRAE

TAIL

**Vertebral Joint**
The vertebrae were
fused to strengthen
the neck.

**Hollow Bones**
made the neck
lighter.

**Ease of Movement**
was made possible
by a ball-and-socket
joint.

**Support**
This area anchored
the supporting
muscles.

LEGS

# A Docile Vegetarian

This striking dinosaur is one of the most widely studied in the history of paleontology. This *quadruped* herbivore could measure up to 29.5 feet (9 m) long and weigh up to 2.2 tons (2 metric tons). Because of its small head, it has been used since the 19th century as a symbol of stupidity. It was later shown that most dinosaurs had small brains and that *Stegosaurus*'s brain was larger than average.

Head

Legs

*Stegosaurus*
▼

Tail

Plates

## STEGOSAURUS

| | |
|---|---|
| Size | 29.5 feet (9 m) |
| Diet | Herbivorous |
| Habitat | Subtropical Forests |
| Epoch | Late Jurassic |
| Range | North America |

**WHERE
IT LIVED**

Dorsal Plate

Caudal Plate

Cervical Plate

# The Cretaceous Period

The dinosaurs continued to diversify, and the first snakes appeared.
The Earth began to look like the planet we know today.
The movement of tectonic plates created folds that
came to form some of the mountain
ranges of today.

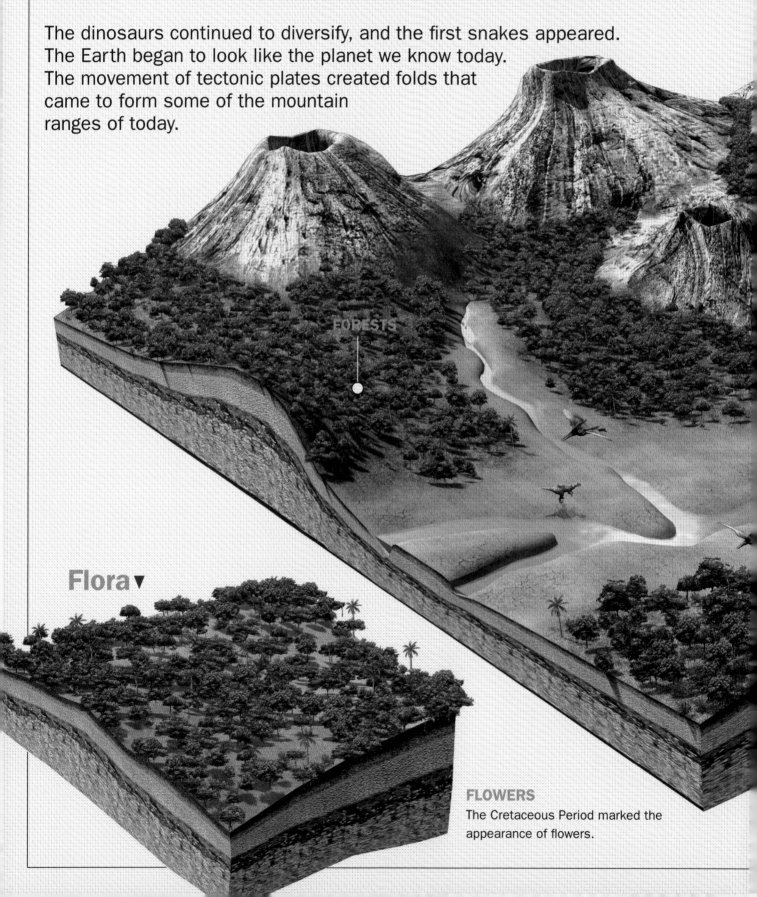

FORESTS

## Flora ▼

**FLOWERS**
The Cretaceous Period marked the
appearance of flowers.

## An Evolving Planet

The Earth now had a warm, mild climate with noticeably different seasons.

# 140 to 65
## million years ago

The Earth began to adopt an appearance similar to that of today. Africa and South America separated from one another, as did North America and Europe. The North and South American plates drifted westward and collided with the Pacific plate, raising both the Rocky Mountains in North America and the Andes in South America.

NORTH AMERICA   EURASIA

AFRICA   INDIA

SOUTH AMERICA

ANTARCTICA

FLYING REPTILES

## Fauna ▶

# A Fierce Era

The Cretaceous Period saw both the splendor and the end of the "Age of Reptiles." It was the longest period of the Mesozoic Era, and for 80 million years, specific types of animal life developed in each region. South America was home to the largest *herbivore* known, *Argentinosaurus huinculensis*, which lived at the same time as the fearsome *theropods*.

## The Struggle to Survive

New groups of dinosaurs emerged during this period. Competition for resources was intense.

*Caudipteryx* ▶

▲
*Suchomimus*

◀
*Corythosaurus*

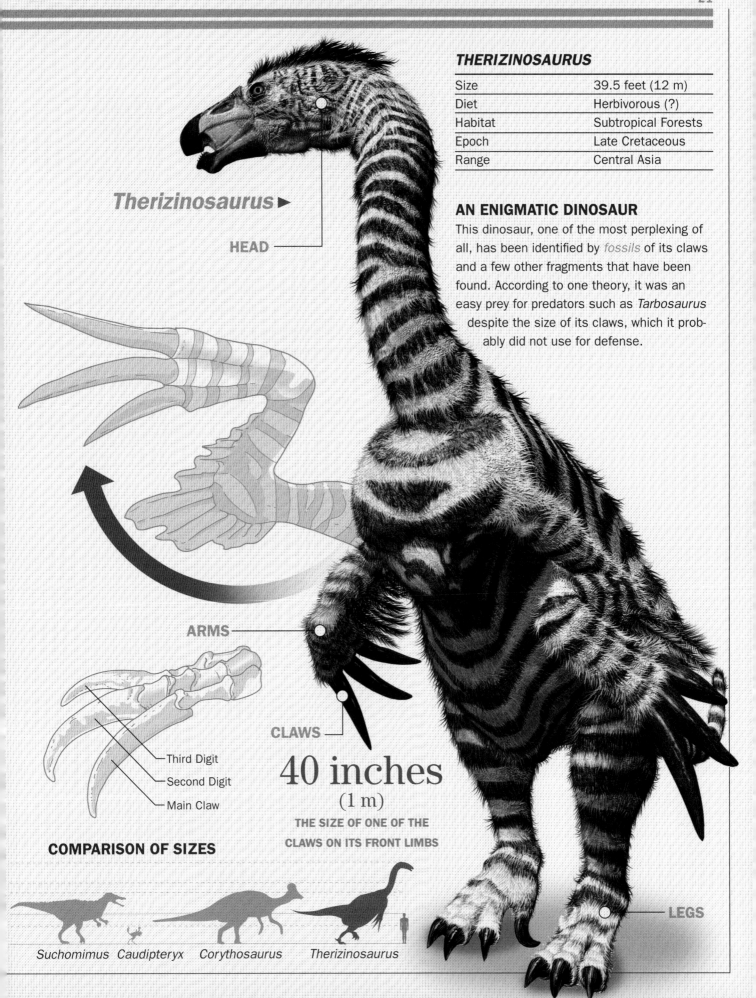

Therizinosaurus ►

HEAD

## THERIZINOSAURUS

| Size | 39.5 feet (12 m) |
|---|---|
| Diet | Herbivorous (?) |
| Habitat | Subtropical Forests |
| Epoch | Late Cretaceous |
| Range | Central Asia |

## AN ENIGMATIC DINOSAUR

This dinosaur, one of the most perplexing of all, has been identified by *fossils* of its claws and a few other fragments that have been found. According to one theory, it was an easy prey for predators such as *Tarbosaurus* despite the size of its claws, which it probably did not use for defense.

ARMS

Third Digit

Second Digit

Main Claw

CLAWS

# 40 inches
## (1 m)

**THE SIZE OF ONE OF THE
CLAWS ON ITS FRONT LIMBS**

## COMPARISON OF SIZES

LEGS

*Suchomimus*   *Caudipteryx*   *Corythosaurus*   *Therizinosaurus*

# The Great Predator of the South

The largest *carnivorous* dinosaur that has ever existed on Earth lived 95 million years ago during the Late Cretaceous Period. *Fossils* of *Giganotosaurus carolinii* were first found in 1993. Although only 70 percent of its skeleton was found, it is known that it could reach a length of up to 49 feet (15 m) and that it hunted large sauropods.

*Giganotosaurus carolinii* ▶

**Powerful Jaws**

**Large Head**

**Claws**

**1** MOVABLE SKULL    **2** LATERAL EXPANSION

A New King

**GIGANOTOSAURUS**

| | |
|---|---|
| Size | 49 feet (15 m) long |
| Diet | Carnivorous |
| Habitat | Forests and Wetlands |
| Epoch | Late Cretaceous |
| Range | South America |

WHERE IT LIVED

Tail

Swift
Hunter

# Living Life to the Limit

Extinctions of living beings on Earth have occurred in a series of drastic episodes throughout history, from the Cambrian Period to the Cretaceous. The most famous chapter is associated with the total disappearance of the dinosaurs about 65.5 million years ago. This mass extinction of these large reptiles is so important that it was used by scientists to indicate the end of the Cretaceous Period and the beginning of the Tertiary, a designation known as the K-T boundary ("K" is the abbreviation for Cretaceous).

## 1 Fatal Meteorites

Some scientists believe mass extinctions were caused by meteorites.

**CLUES IN CHICXULUB**

POST-EXTINCTION LAYER

FIREBALL LAYER

EJECTION LAYER

PRE-EXTINCTION LAYER

**MIXED ROCKS**

Samples taken from the Chicxulub crater show a mixture of terrestrial minerals (dark areas) and meteorite minerals (light areas).

**50%**
OF ALL SPECIES BECAME EXTINCT AT THE K-T BOUNDARY.

**LOCATION OF CRATER**

Outer Edge of the Crater

Yucatán Channel

CUBA

Campeche Bay

Cancún

Mérida

MEXICO

Guatemala

| 0 | 100 | 200 miles |
|---|---|---|
| (0 | 160 | 320 km) |

## ② Volcanoes

Frequent eruptions may have caused extinctions.

## ③ Meteorites

Meteoroids and comets from the Oort cloud may have contributed.

## ④ Other Proposed Theories

Some scientists believe a combination of events led to mass extinctions.

# 6 miles
### (10 km)

**DIAMETER OF THE ASTEROID THAT CAUSED THE CHICXULUB CRATER IN MEXICO**

# 50
## million

**ATOMIC BOMBS LIKE THE ONE DROPPED ON HIROSHIMA EQUAL THE FORCE OF THE IMPACT OF ONE METEORITE MEASURING 6 MILES (10 KM) IN DIAMETER.**

# 112 miles (180 km)

**DIAMETER OF THE CHICXULUB CRATER ON THE YUCATÁN PENINSULA**

# The Family Tree

The first reptiles descended from ancestral *amphibians*. They distinguished themselves from their ancestors through mutations that allowed them to free themselves from their dependence on water for reproduction. Among these adaptations, the amniotic egg stands out, but equally important were the development of sex organs that favored internal copulation, and an impermeable skin. These adaptations to its environment were necessary to the reptilian dominance of the greater part of the Mesozoic Era.

**TEETH**

**REPTILE** *EVOLUTION*

*Ichthyosaurs*

MARINE REPTILES

Lizards

*Metriorhynchus*

CROCODILIANS

SAUROPTERYGIANS

*Scutosaurus*

*Hylonomus*

SNAKES, LIZARDS, AND SPHENODONTS

CAPTORHINIDS AND *HYLONOMUS*

*ARCHOSAURUS*
Antorbital fenestra

Diapsid skull

*Archelon*

ANAPSIDS

Canine teeth in the upper mandible

REPTILES

**FEET**

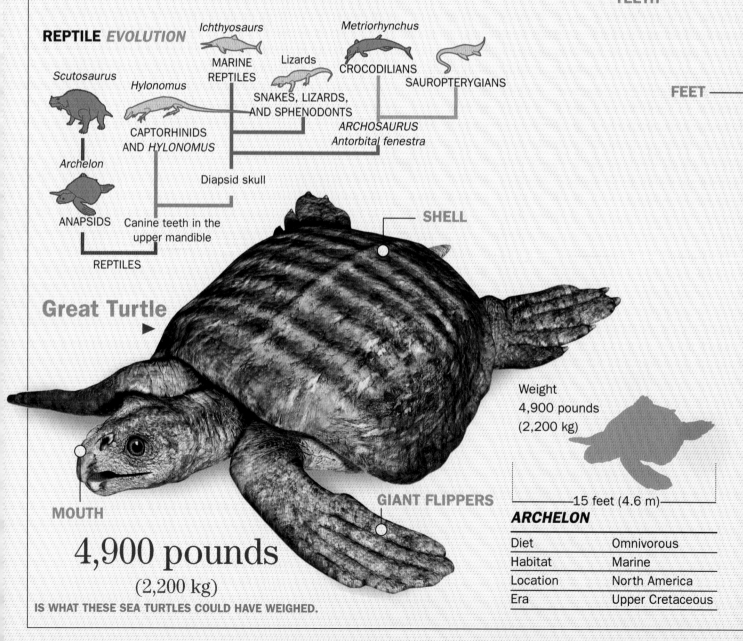

**SHELL**

**Great Turtle** ▶

**MOUTH**

**GIANT FLIPPERS**

Weight
4,900 pounds
(2,200 kg)

——15 feet (4.6 m)——

## 4,900 pounds
### (2,200 kg)
**IS WHAT THESE SEA TURTLES COULD HAVE WEIGHED.**

**ARCHELON**

| | |
|---|---|
| Diet | Omnivorous |
| Habitat | Marine |
| Location | North America |
| Era | Upper Cretaceous |

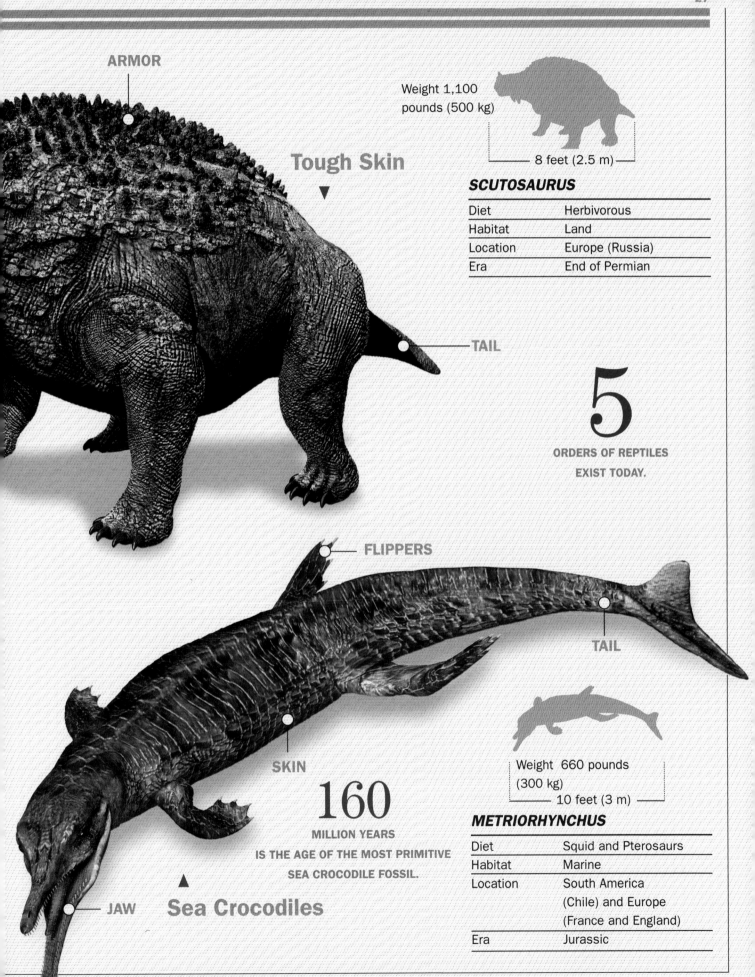

ARMOR

Tough Skin ▼

Weight 1,100 pounds (500 kg)

8 feet (2.5 m)

### SCUTOSAURUS

| | |
|---|---|
| Diet | Herbivorous |
| Habitat | Land |
| Location | Europe (Russia) |
| Era | End of Permian |

TAIL

## 5

ORDERS OF REPTILES

EXIST TODAY.

FLIPPERS

TAIL

SKIN

Weight 660 pounds (300 kg)

10 feet (3 m)

### METRIORHYNCHUS

| | |
|---|---|
| Diet | Squid and Pterosaurs |
| Habitat | Marine |
| Location | South America (Chile) and Europe (France and England) |
| Era | Jurassic |

## 160

MILLION YEARS

IS THE AGE OF THE MOST PRIMITIVE

SEA CROCODILE FOSSIL.

JAW ▲ Sea Crocodiles

# A Skin with Scales

Reptile skin is hard, dry, and flaky. The first reptiles appeared during the height of the Carboniferous Period in the Paleozoic Era. During the Mesozoic Era, they *evolved* and flourished, which is why this period is also known as the age of reptiles. Only 5 of the 23 orders that existed then have living representatives today.

▲ **Solomon Island Skink**

EYES

NICTITATING MEMBRANE

## 4,765
**SPECIES OF LIZARDS EXIST.**

## Reptiles Habitat

▲ **Black Caiman**

## Crocodiles

THORAX AND ABDOMEN

▲ **American Alligator**

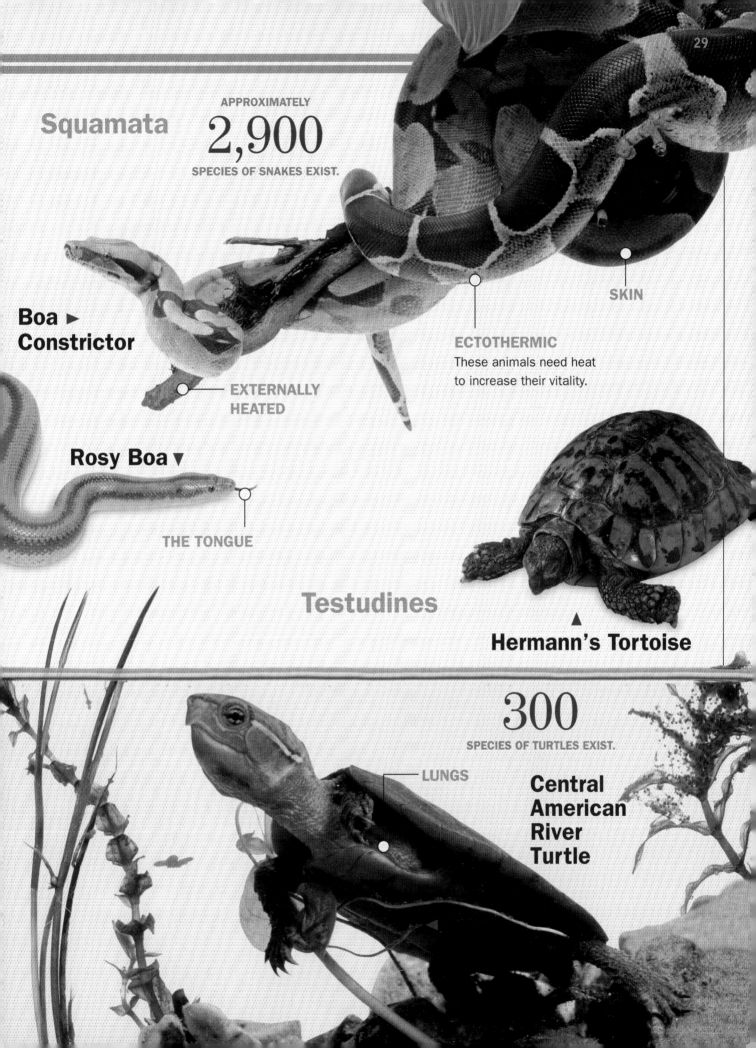

# Squamata

APPROXIMATELY

## 2,900

SPECIES OF SNAKES EXIST.

**Boa ►**
**Constrictor**

SKIN

ECTOTHERMIC
These animals need heat
to increase their vitality.

EXTERNALLY
HEATED

**Rosy Boa ▼**

THE TONGUE

# Testudines

**Hermann's Tortoise** ▲

## 300

SPECIES OF TURTLES EXIST.

LUNGS

**Central
American
River
Turtle**

# Reproduction

Most reptiles are oviparous. Some species lay large numbers of eggs and then allow them to develop on their own, generally in well-protected nests or hidden under dirt or sand. Marine turtles, especially green turtles, travel to the coast to lay their eggs in the sand, where they are left at the mercy of all who pass by. The females of other species, however, fiercely protect their offspring, staying near their nests for long periods of time to scare away potential *predators*.

**Green Anaconda** ▼

## Eggshells

**①** **Growth**

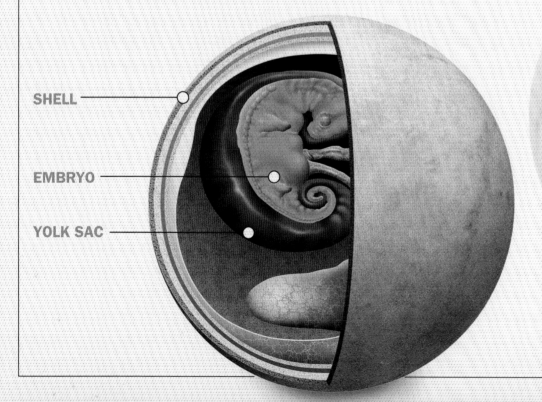

SHELL

EMBRYO

YOLK SAC

**②** **Fracture**

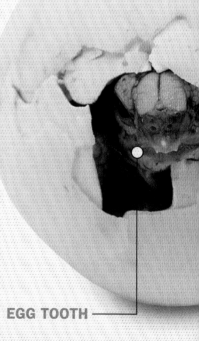

EGG TOOTH

# 145 to 160 days

**IS THE INCUBATION PERIOD OF THE LEOPARD TORTOISE.**

**④ Exit**

MOUTH

FOOT

CARAPACE (SHELL)

**❸ Hatching**

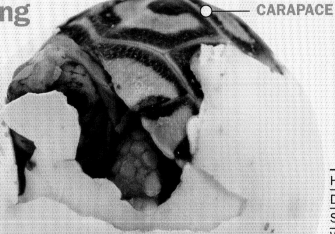

CARAPACE

**LEOPARD TORTOISE**

| Habitat | Africa |
| --- | --- |
| Diet | Herbivorous |
| Size | 23-26 inches (60-65 cm) |
| Weight | 77 pounds (35 kg) |

**Fer-de-Lance**
▼

**CONSISTENCY OF THE EGGS**

Hard    Soft

# Lizards

Lizards are the largest group of reptiles. They live in most environments except for extremely cold regions. There are land-dwelling, underground, tree-dwelling, and even semi-aquatic lizards. They can walk, climb, dig, run, and even glide. Lizards often have differentiated heads, movable eyelids, a rigid lower jaw, four five-toed feet, a long body covered with *scales*, and a long tail. Some can even shed their tails when threatened.

## CAMOUFLAGE

IS AN ADAPTIVE ADVANTAGE. BY BLENDING IN WITH THE VEGETATION SURROUNDING THEM, LIZARDS CAN ESCAPE THE NOTICE OF BOTH THEIR *PREDATORS* AND THEIR PREY.

**Day Geckos** ▼

**STICKY TOES**

## Geckos and Skinks

**LIFESAVING RECOURSE**

## Chameleons

**TELESCOPIC EYES**

**SKIN**

**TAIL**

**PREHENSILE TOES**

▲ **Meller's Chameleon**

**CLAW**

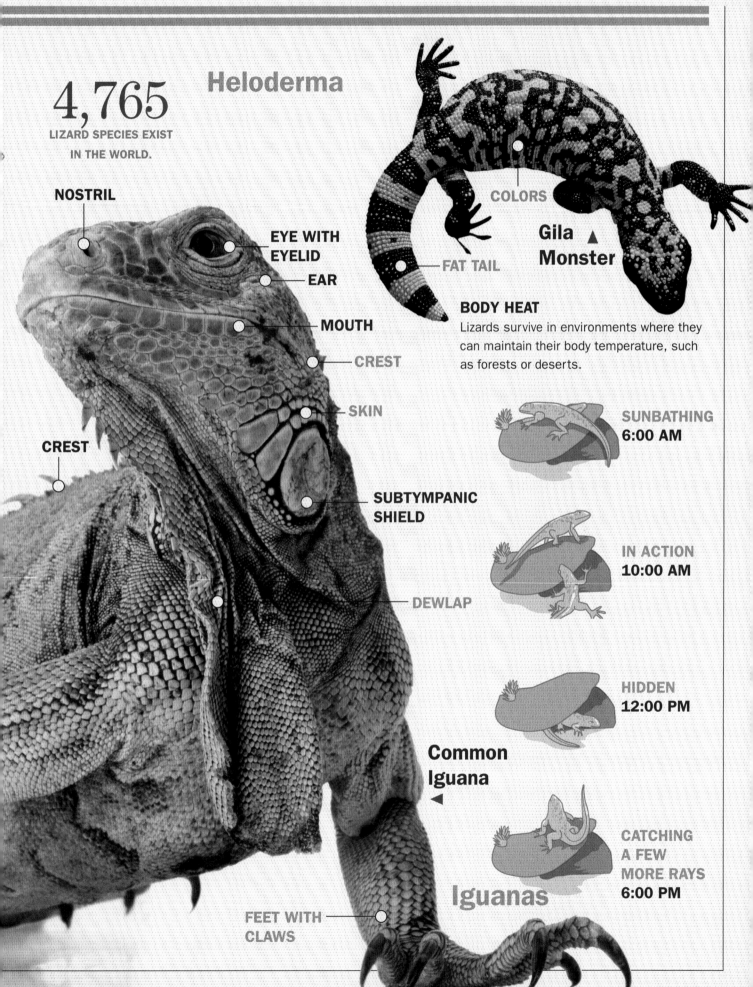

**4,765**
LIZARD SPECIES EXIST
IN THE WORLD.

Heloderma

NOSTRIL

EYE WITH
EYELID

EAR

MOUTH

CREST

SKIN

CREST

SUBTYMPANIC
SHIELD

DEWLAP

FEET WITH
CLAWS

COLORS

FAT TAIL

Gila ▲
Monster

**BODY HEAT**
Lizards survive in environments where they
can maintain their body temperature, such
as forests or deserts.

SUNBATHING
6:00 AM

IN ACTION
10:00 AM

HIDDEN
12:00 PM

**Common
Iguana**
◄

CATCHING
A FEW
MORE RAYS
6:00 PM

Iguanas

# Komodo Dragon

This animal is the largest lizard in the world. It is related to monitor lizards and can grow up to 9.8 feet (3 m) long and weigh up to approximately 330 pounds (150 kg). These endangered lizards live only on a group of islands in Indonesia. They are *carnivorous* and are known for their ferocity in attacking their prey. Their saliva is full of bacteria that can kill their prey with only one bite. They can detect other Komodo dragons from several miles away.

INDONESIA

**Komodo National Park**

Banta

Sumbawa

Padar

Nusa

Komodo

Rinca

Kode   Montong

TOUGH SKIN

CLAWS

STOMACH

**SIZE AND WEIGHT**

Males can grow more than 10 feet long. Females are somewhat smaller.

6 feet (1.8 m)

Weight  330 pounds (150 kg)
—9.8 feet (3 m)—
Komodo Dragon

Weight  22 pounds (10 kg)
—3.3 feet (1 m)—
Iguana

Weight 175 pounds (80 kg)
Human

# How It Attacks Its Prey

## 5,000

**LIZARDS OF THE FAMILY VARANIDAE LIVE IN THE WILD ON SIX SMALL INDONESIAN ISLANDS, INCLUDING KOMODO ISLAND.**

**A LONG HUNT**

Komodo dragons have an acute sense of smell that can detect the presence of other animals up to 2 miles (3 km) away. They track their prey using their forked tongues to detect scents.

**1 SEARCH**

SMELL

**2 BITE**

SALIVA

TONGUE

**3 FEEDING**

**4 STRUGGLE**

## Deadly Saliva

*PASTEURELLA MULTOCIDA*
Bacteria that affects the gastrointestinal and respiratory tracts of mammals and birds

# Changing Colors

Chameleons are well known for their ability to change color. Another interesting fact is that their tongue can stretch great distances in seconds. They live mostly in Africa. Their prehensile tails and toes make them excellent climbers. Another helpful characteristic is that their eyes can move independently of one another, providing them a 360° field of vision. Their flat bodies help them to balance and to hide among the leaves.

**PREHENSILE TAIL**

Protractible Tongue

1 Contraction

## How It Changes Color

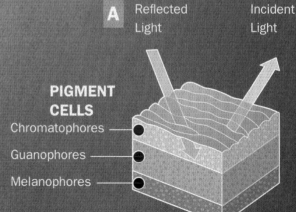

**A**   Reflected Light     Incident Light

**PIGMENT CELLS**
- Chromatophores
- Guanophores
- Melanophores

**PANTHER CHAMELEON**

| Range | Madagascar |
| Habitat | Coastal Regions |
| Lifestyle | Diurnal |

## Feeding Habits

TONGUE

TIP

## ② Unfolding

## ③ Retraction

**B** Reflected Light

Incident Light

**FEET**

2 Toes

3 Toes

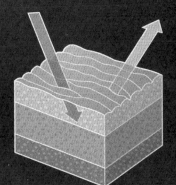

# Venerated and Feared

Crocodiles, alligators, caimans, and gavials are very ancient animals. They have changed very little in the last 65 million years. They can go for long periods without moving; during these times, they sun themselves or rest in the water. However, they can also swim, jump, and even run at high speed to attack with force and precision.

**LOWER JAW**

**SCALES**

**GAVIAL**

**GAVIAL**

**CROCODILE**

**ALLIGATOR**

| Habitat | Freshwater |
|---|---|
| Number of Types | One |
| Degree of Danger | Harmless |

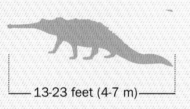

— 13-23 feet (4-7 m) —

## The Gavial
▼

**SNOUT**

**TEETH**

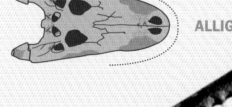

**1 FORWARD**

**2 LEGS SUSPENDED**

**3 REPEAT**

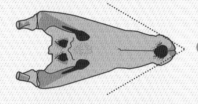

## 9 miles per hour (15 km/h)
**IS THE SPEED THEY CAN REACH AT A FULL RUN.**

# Ocean Species

**SHELL**

**Hawksbill Turtle ▶**

**HEAD**

**SIDE-NECKED TURTLE**

## CONCEALED FROM DANGER

Many scientists believe that turtles' shells enabled them to survive long ago, during a time when so many other reptile species, including dinosaurs, perished.

**STRAIGHT-NECKED TURTLE**

**HEAD**

**LEGS AND TAIL**

**LEGS AND TAIL**

**SHELL**

## A TURTLE'S AGE

Counting the successive hornlike plates that grow on the shell each year allows us to determine a turtle's age.

**▲Hermann's Tortoise**

**PLASTRON**

## On Solid Ground

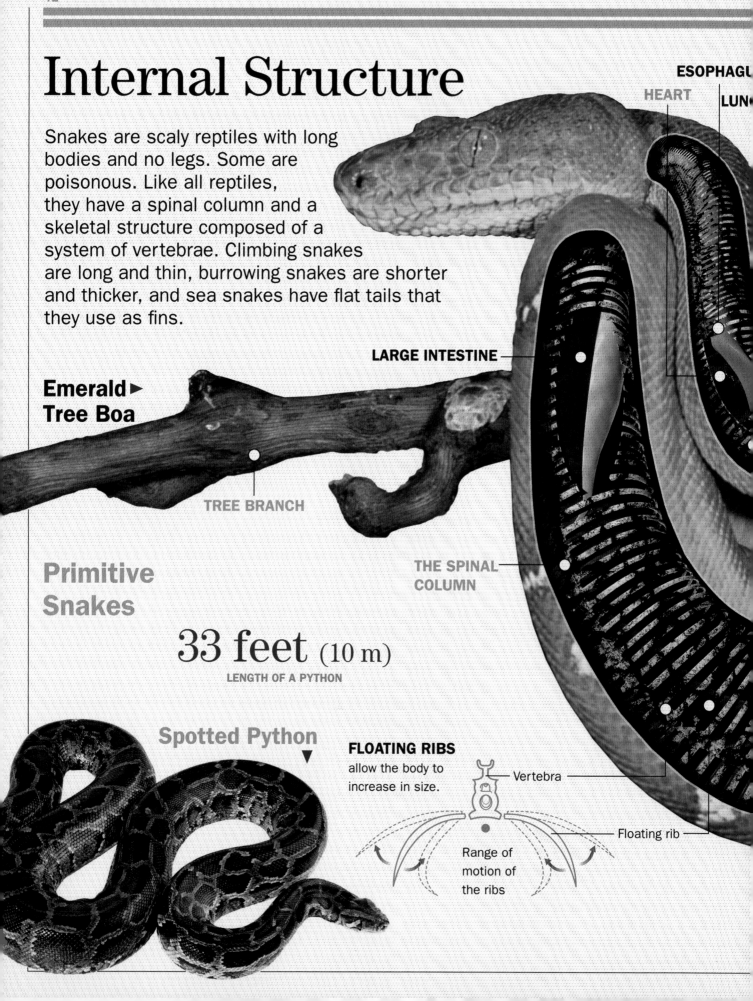

# Internal Structure

Snakes are scaly reptiles with long bodies and no legs. Some are poisonous. Like all reptiles, they have a spinal column and a skeletal structure composed of a system of vertebrae. Climbing snakes are long and thin, burrowing snakes are shorter and thicker, and sea snakes have flat tails that they use as fins.

**Emerald ▶ Tree Boa**

**ESOPHAGU**

**HEART**

**LUN**

**LARGE INTESTINE**

**TREE BRANCH**

**THE SPINAL COLUMN**

**Primitive Snakes**

## 33 feet (10 m)
**LENGTH OF A PYTHON**

**Spotted Python** ▼

**FLOATING RIBS** allow the body to increase in size.

Vertebra

Floating rib

Range of motion of the ribs

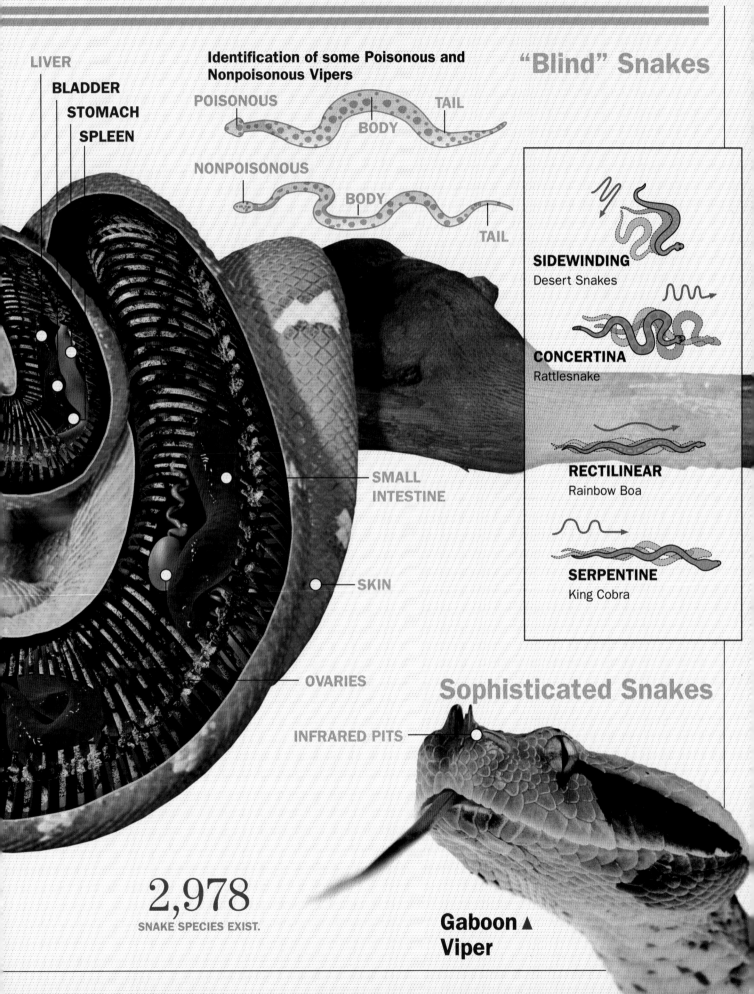

LIVER

BLADDER

STOMACH

SPLEEN

## Identification of some Poisonous and Nonpoisonous Vipers

POISONOUS

TAIL

BODY

NONPOISONOUS

BODY

TAIL

## "Blind" Snakes

**SIDEWINDING**
Desert Snakes

**CONCERTINA**
Rattlesnake

**RECTILINEAR**
Rainbow Boa

**SERPENTINE**
King Cobra

SMALL INTESTINE

SKIN

OVARIES

## Sophisticated Snakes

INFRARED PITS

## 2,978
SNAKE SPECIES EXIST.

**Gaboon ▲ Viper**

# Cobras

Easily recognized by their outspread hoods, cobras are well known worldwide, mostly because of their use by snake charmers. Many cobra species carry deadly *venom*. Some can even spit from several yards away. Cobras of the *Naja* genus are the most widely recognized. They are widespread in Asia and were only recently recognized as 11 separate species. All are *predatory*.

**Red Spitting Cobra ▼**

SMOOTH SCALES

BLACK BAND

## How To Distinguish Among Them

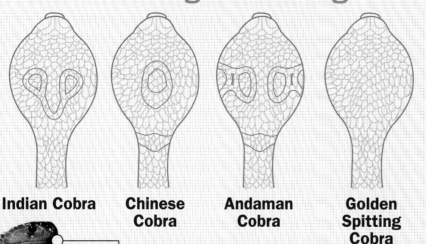

**Indian Cobra**  **Chinese Cobra**  **Andaman Cobra**  **Golden Spitting Cobra**

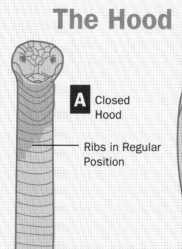

VENOM

◄ **Asian Cobra**

BANDS

## The Hood

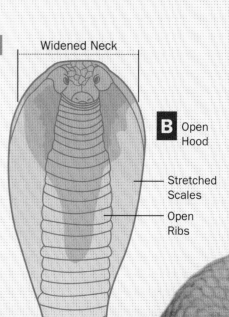

Widened Neck

**A** Closed Hood

Ribs in Regular Position

**B** Open Hood

Stretched Scales

Open Ribs

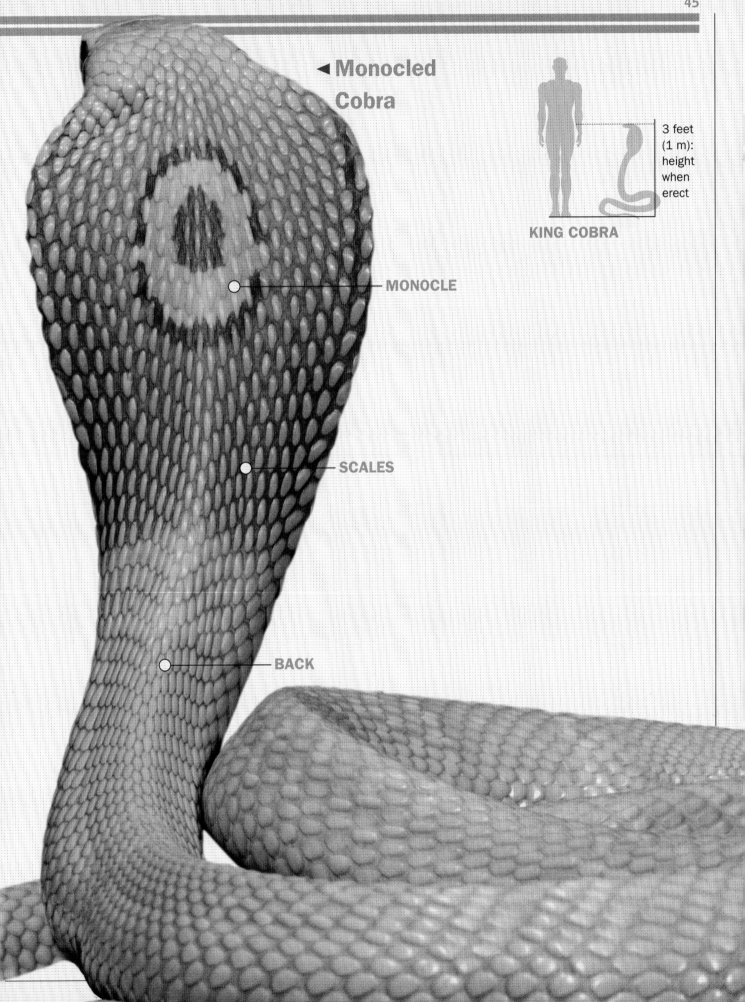

◄ **Monocled Cobra**

3 feet (1 m): height when erect

**KING COBRA**

MONOCLE

SCALES

BACK

# Fewer Each Time

Many species of reptiles are at serious risk of extinction—mostly because of habitat loss caused by human activities. The most threatened species with the fewest resources for recovery are those native to islands. Urban growth, deforestation, and water contamination are among the principal forces that have created this critical situation. Conscious of the problem, many countries have developed legislation to protect reptiles, but it is not always effective.

## ARUBA ISLAND RATTLESNAKE

| Status | Critical |
|---|---|
| Habitat | Aruba |
| Size | 3 feet (95 cm) |

## GOLDEN FER-DE-LANCE

| Status | Critical |
|---|---|
| Habitat | Brazil |
| Size | 2.6 feet (80 cm) |

**Aruba Island Rattlesnake**

**Fiji Crested Iguana**

## BULGARDAGH VIPER

| Status | Critical |
|---|---|
| Habitat | Turkey |
| Size | 2.6 feet (80 cm) |

## FIJI CRESTED IGUANA

| Status | Critical |
|---|---|
| Habitat | Fiji |
| Size | 2.5 feet (75 cm) |

## Habitat Loss
**THE LOSS OF HABITAT CAUSED BY HUMAN ACTIVITIES IS THE MAIN CAUSE OF REPTILE EXTINCTION.**

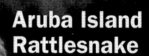

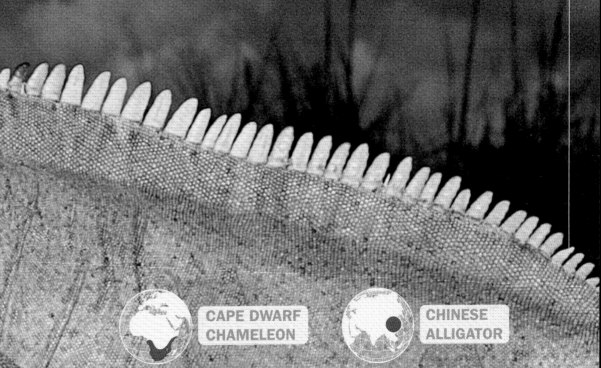

 **HIERRO
GIANT
LIZARD**

| Status | Critical |
|---|---|
| Habitat | **Canary Islands** |
| Maximum Size | **2 feet (60 cm)** |

 **JAMAICA
RACER**

| Status | Critical |
|---|---|
| Habitat | **Jamaica** |
| Size | **2.8 feet (85 cm)** |

 **TURKS AND
CAICOS
ROCK
IGUANA**

| Status | Critical |
|---|---|
| Habitat | **Bahamas** |
| Size | **14 inches (36 cm)** |

 **CAPE DWARF
CHAMELEON**

| Status | Critical |
|---|---|
| Habitat | **South Africa** |
| Maximum Size | **8 inches (20 cm)** |

**CHINESE
ALLIGATOR**

| Status | Critical |
|---|---|
| Habitat | **China** |
| Maximum Size | **6 feet (2 m)** |

# Origin

The *evolution* of birds is a debated theme in science. The most widespread theory states that birds descend from *theropods*, dinosaurs that walked on two legs. *Fossils* of dinosaur specimens with *feathers* have been found, but *Archaeopteryx*, a primitive bird that lived 150 million years ago, is the oldest relative known. Completely covered with feathers, it had a pair of wings that enabled it to fly. However, it retained many dinosaur traits.

**ARCHAEOPTERYX LITHOGRAPHICA**

lived in the Jurassic Period, 150 million years ago.

Comparison to a Human

| Diet | Carnivore |
|---|---|
| Length | 10 inches (25 cm) |
| Height | 8 to 12 inches (20-30 cm) |
| Weight | 18 ounces (500 g) |

**REPTILIAN JAWBONES WITH TEETH**

**SPINE**

## From Reptile to Bird

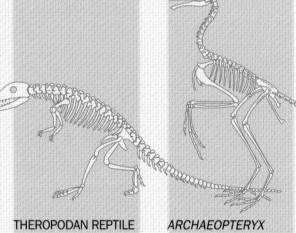

THEROPODAN REPTILE
From the Triassic Period

*ARCHAEOPTERYX*
From the Jurassic Period

PIGEON
Alive Today

Brain

*Archaeopteryx*

**SKULL**

**Modern Bird**

## Fossils

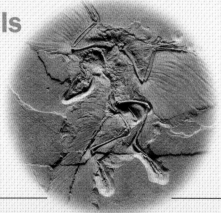

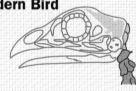

**FROM ARMS TO WINGS**

It had a greater range of motion in the upper limbs than primitive dinosaurs.

***ARCHAEOPTERYX***
**150 million years ago**

**Talons for climbing trees**

**THREE TOES WITH TALONS**

**WRIST**

**FURCULA**

**RIBS**

**SAURIAN PELVIS**

**VERTEBRATE TAIL**

During flight, it functioned as a rudder. On the ground, it provided balance for walking.

**TOES**

Its movements were limited by its shoulder joint, which was placed forward.

**VELOCIRAPTOR**
**99 to 65 million years ago**

Birds have greater mobility than *Archaeopteryx*.

**PIGEON**
**modern**

# Adaptations

There are three main theories to explain why birds developed the ability to fly. The evidence that supports each of them tells a story of adaptations to an aerial world in which the fight for food and survival is key. One reasonable theory argues that birds descended from an extinct line of *biped* reptiles that fed on plants and used to jump from branch to branch to flee.

## Today

**THE TIPS OF THE WINGS PROPEL FLIGHT, THE ARMS SUPPORT THE BIRD, AND THE SHOULDERS ENABLE THE FLAPPING MOVEMENTS.**

**150** million years ago

Highly Mobile Shoulder

Emergence of the Tarsometatarsus

**175** million years ago

Rotary Shoulder

Three Fingers

**200** million years ago

Limited Shoulder

Five Fingers

Short Arm

## The Emergence of the Wing

## From Reptile to Bird

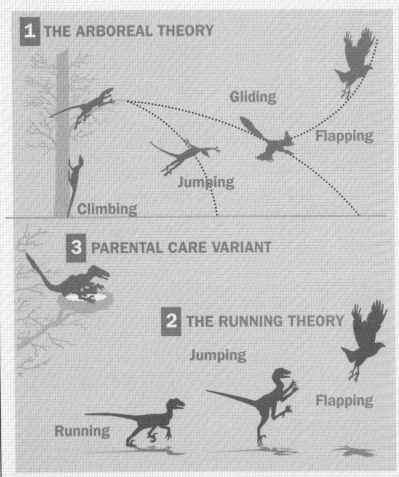

**1** THE ARBOREAL THEORY

Gliding

Flapping

Jumping

Climbing

**3** PARENTAL CARE VARIANT

**2** THE RUNNING THEORY

Jumping

Flapping

Running

**GLIDING SPECIES**

Flying Squirrel

Flying Gecko

**OTHER FLYING ANIMALS**

**FEATHERS:
THE BEST SOLUTION**

**4** FEATHERS

**3** MODIFIED SCALES

**26 pounds**
**(12 kg)**
IS THE MAXIMUM WEIGHT
AN EAGLE CAN CARRY
DURING FLIGHT.

LARGE SCALES **2**

**EAGLE**
In its maneuvers,
this great hunter
displays the entire
*evolution* of flight.

**From Scales
to Feathers**

**1** SCALES

# One Bird, One Name

The people who developed scientific thought created a classification system that took into consideration the external form as well as the behavior of birds; hence, the denominations predator, wading bird, and songbird were developed, among others. The most recent system of classification, which is based on genetic and evolutionary criteria, has generated an organization of names that is constantly being updated.

**Hoatzin** ▲

## What Is a Classification?

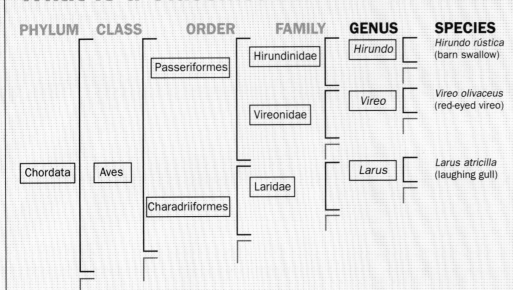

| PHYLUM | CLASS | ORDER | FAMILY | GENUS | SPECIES |
|--------|-------|-------|--------|-------|---------|
| | | Passeriformes | Hirundinidae | *Hirundo* | *Hirundo rústica* (barn swallow) |
| | | | Vireonidae | *Vireo* | *Vireo olivaceus* (red-eyed vireo) |
| Chordata | Aves | Charadriiformes | Laridae | *Larus* | *Larus atricilla* (laughing gull) |

**APODIFORMES**
**431 SPECIES**
Hummingbirds and Swifts

**CAPRIMULGIFORMES**
**109 SPECIES**
Potoos, Frogmouths, and Nightjars

**SPHENISCIFORMES**
**18 SPECIES**
Penguins

**PROCELLARIIFORMES**
**110 SPECIES**
Albatrosses, Petrels, and Fulmars

**GAVIIFORMES**
**5 SPECIES**
Loons (diving birds)

**PODICIPEDIFORMES**
**21 SPECIES**
Grebes

**ANSERIFORMES**
**150 SPECIES**
Ducks, Geese, and Swans

**PELECANIFORMES**
**62 SPECIES**
Pelicans, Boobies, and Cormorants

# Diversity and the Environment

Living birds are distributed among a wide variety of habitats.

**FALCONIFORMES**
**295 SPECIES**
Condors, Buzzards, Eagles, Vultures, and Falcons

**COLIIFORMES**
**6 SPECIES**
Mousebirds

**CUCULIFORMES**
**160 SPECIES**
Cuckoos, Turacos, and Hoatzins

**COLUMBIFORMES**
**317 SPECIES**
Pigeons and Doves

**PSITTACIFORMES**
**360 SPECIES**
Parrots, Parakeets, Lories, Cockatoos, and Macaws

**CORACIIFORMES**
**204 SPECIES**
Common Kingfishers and Bee-Eaters

**PASSERIFORMES**
**5,400 SPECIES**
Perching Birds and Songbirds

**PICIFORMES**
**382 SPECIES**
Woodpeckers, Toucans, and Puffbirds

**CHARADRIIFORMES**
**350 SPECIES**
Seagulls, Lapwings, and Plovers

**UPUPIFORMES**
**1 SPECIES**
Hoopoe

**STRIGIFORMES**
**174 SPECIES**
Owls

**CICONIIFORMES**
**120 SPECIES**
Herons, Storks, Ibises, and Egrets

**GRUIFORMES**
**190 SPECIES**
Moorhens, Cranes, and Coots

**TROGONIFORMES**
**39 SPECIES**
Trogons and Quetzals

**STRUTHIONIFORMES**
**1 SPECIES**
Ostrich

**PHOENICOPTERIFORMES**
**1 SPECIES**
Flamingos

**CASUARIIFORMES**
**4 SPECIES**
Cassowaries and Emus

**APTERYGIFORMES**
**4 SPECIES**
Kiwis

**GALLIFORMES**
**274 SPECIES**
Chickens, Turkeys, Quails, Pheasants, and Partridges

**TINAMIFORMES**
**47 SPECIES**
Tinamous

**RHEIFORMES**
**2 SPECIES**
Rheas

# Beyond Feathers

A bird is an animal covered with *feathers* that has a toothless *bill* and limbs morphed into wings. Other distinguishing characteristics are that they are warm-blooded and have pneumatic bones—bones filled with air chambers instead of marrow. Birds have very efficient circulatory and respiratory systems and great neuromuscular and sensory coordination.

## Variety and Uniformity

Birds can be found in aquatic, aerial, terrestrial, polar, and tropical zones.

**WINE-THROATED HUMMINGBIRD**

## 0.06 ounce (1.6 g)

**WEIGHT OF THE SMALLEST BIRD**

**AFRICAN OSTRICH**

## 330 pounds
### (150 kg)
**THE WEIGHT OF THE LARGEST BIRD**

## Adaptation to Flying

No other living animal has feathers. They are appealing for their structure and variety.

**PENGUIN**

### -75° F
### (-60° C)
**THE TEMPERATURE PENGUINS CAN ENDURE IN ANTARCTICA**

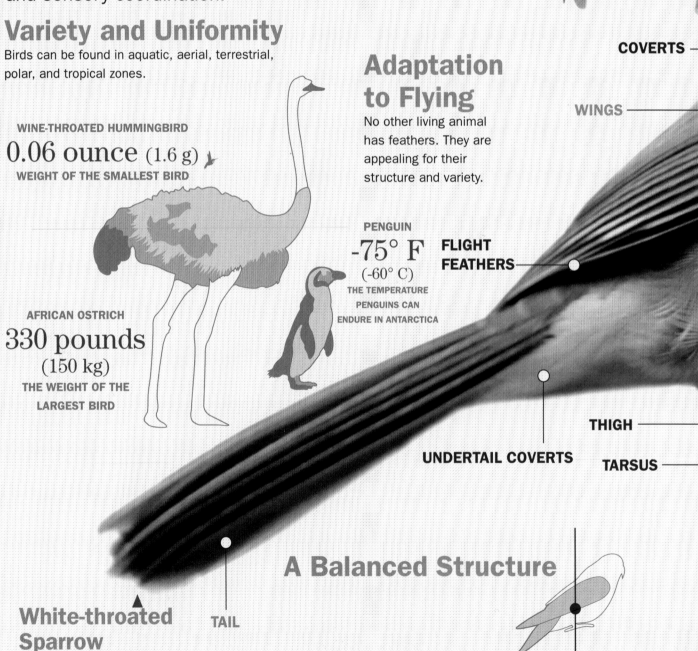

**COVERTS**

**WINGS**

**FLIGHT FEATHERS**

**THIGH**

**TARSUS**

**UNDERTAIL COVERTS**

## A Balanced Structure

**White-throated Sparrow**

**TAIL**

PREMAXILLA

# Hardness

Its long, stout bill is extraordinarily hard. Despite its appearance, the bill is very light, and birds can use it adeptly to seize and to open the fruits they eat.

UPPER MAXILLARY BONE

CULMEN

LOWER MAXILLARY BONE

DENTARY

TIP

## The Shape of the Bill

TOUCANS AND ARICARI

FLAMINGO

HERON

GREENFINCH

FALCON

RAVEN

HUMMINGBIRD

CROSSBILL

# Exposed Legs

Looking at the extremities of birds, including their toes and claws, can help us learn about their behavior. Their characteristics reveal information about the environments in which different groups of birds live, as well as about their diets. The shape and placement of bones, muscles, and tendons make it possible to understand how birds hold their prey or perch on branches, as well as to learn about the mechanics of their movement across the ground and in the water.

## Different Types of Feet

**FEET DESIGNED FOR SEIZING**

**FEET DESIGNED FOR CLIMBING**

**FEET DESIGNED FOR WALKING**

**FEET DESIGNED FOR PERCHING**

**FEET DESIGNED FOR SWIMMING**

**FEET DESIGNED FOR RUNNING**

**ADAPTATION TO TREES**

# Claws, Scales, and Spurs

These striking foot structures play a role in movement protection, defense, and finding food.

**BALD EAGLE (TALONS)**

**GREAT CRESTED GREBE (LOBED TOES)**

**Tricolored Heron**

THIGH

ANKLE

## Leg Structures

**BIRD LEG**

Thigh

Knee

Tibia

Tarsus and Metatarsus

Heel

Foot

Hallux

Toes

**HUMAN LEG**

Thigh

Knee

Tibia

Heel

Metatarsus

Toes

Tarsus

Foot

**SCOTS DUMPY ROOSTER (SPURS)**

# Tail Types

Over the course of *evolution*, birds' tail vertebrae fused into a pygostyle, and in their place feathers of different sizes and colors emerged. These feathers can control aerial maneuvers during flight, work as brakes during landing, and make noise. Males also use them during *courtship* to dazzle and win over females.

## The Key to How It Works

The tail can perform a variety of functions because of the movement and shape of the feathers. The powerful muscles in the pygostyle prepare the plumage for courtship displays and for flight, provide balance in walking and alighting on trees, and work as rudders for swimming.

**OPEN**  **CLOSED**  **OPEN**

LANDING I  LANDING II  LANDING III

## Courtship Display

A grouse will display its tail feathers during courtship.

OPEN CLOSED

RECTRICES

UNDERTAIL COVERTS

## Fan of Rectrices

FORKED TAIL ROUNDED TAIL

Black Grouse

GRADUATED TAIL

MARGINATED TAIL

SQUARE TAIL

# Feathers

Feathers are the feature that distinguishes birds from all other animals. They make birds strikingly colorful, protect them against cold and intense heat, enable them to move easily through the air and water, and hide them from enemies. A bird's set of feathers is called its plumage, and its color is essential for reproductive success.

## Structure

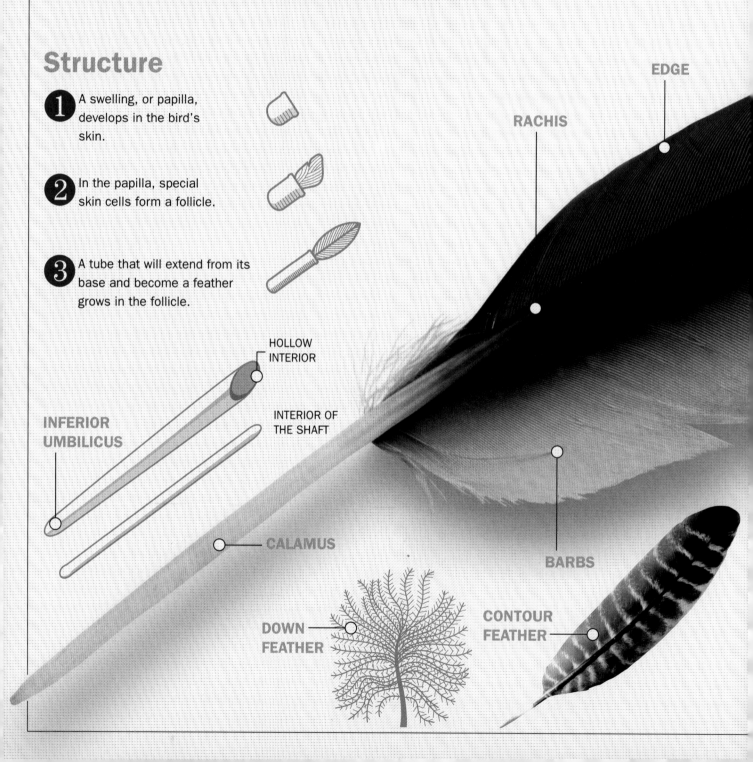

**1** A swelling, or papilla, develops in the bird's skin.

**2** In the papilla, special skin cells form a follicle.

**3** A tube that will extend from its base and become a feather grows in the follicle.

EDGE

RACHIS

HOLLOW INTERIOR

INTERIOR OF THE SHAFT

INFERIOR UMBILICUS

CALAMUS

BARBS

DOWN FEATHER

CONTOUR FEATHER

TRAILING
EDGE NOTCH

Barbs

Barbules

Hooklets, or
Barbicels

VANE, OR BLADE

Imperial
Heron
▶

POWDER DOWN

# Types of Feathers

SPECIAL
FEATHERS

Vibrissae

Filoplumes

SEASONAL CHANGE

**Ptarmigan**

SUMMER
PLUMAGE

WINTER
PLUMAGE

PLUMAGE MOLTING

# Wings to Fly

Wings are highly modified arms that, through their unique structure and shape, enable most birds to fly. Among all wings that have existed in the animal kingdom, those of birds are the best for flying. Their wings are light and durable, and in some cases their shape and effectiveness can be modified during flight. To understand the relationship between wings and a bird's weight, the concept of wing loading, which helps explain the type of flight for each species, is useful.

## Wings in the Animal Kingdom

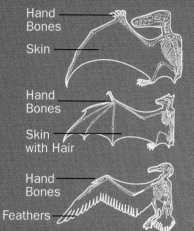

Hand Bones — PTERODACTYLS
Skin —

Hand Bones — BATS
Skin with Hair —

Hand Bones — BIRDS
Feathers —

## Types of Wings

The external primary feathers are longer.

The outermost primary feathers are shorter than the central ones.

They are wide at the base, with separate feather tips.

There are many secondary feathers.

Short feathers are located all over the wing.

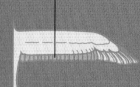

FAST WING

ELLIPTICAL WINGS

WINGS FOR SOARING ABOVE LAND

WINGS FOR SOARING ABOVE THE OCEAN

WINGS FOR SWIMMING

FUNCTION

**Wing Size and Loading**

11.5 ft
(3.5 m)

**WANDERING ALBATROSS**

24 ft
(7.3 m)

*ARGENTAVIS MAGNIFICENS*
(Extinct)

5 ft
(1.5 m)

LARGER FINGER

SMALLER FINGER

CARPOMETACARPUS

ALULAR DIGIT
Controls the alula, a feathered projection on the front edge of the wing.

ULNA

RADIUS

HUMERUS

CORACOID

STERNUM
OR KEEL

**GREATER WING COVERTS**

PRIMARIES

PRIMARY COVERTS

MEDIAN WING COVERTS

SECONDARIES

TERTIARIES

LOOSE FEATHERS

PRIMARY FEATHERS

**Flightless Wings**

FUNCTION

# Flight

Most flying birds use flapping flight all the time. It consists of moving through the air as if rowing with the wings. With each flap (raising and lowering), the wing both sustains the bird in the air and pushes its body forward. There are different types of flapping flight and different rates of flapping. In general, the larger the bird, the more powerful and less frequent its flapping will be. Birds that cover long distances have long, narrow wings; those that fly among trees have short, rounded wings.

**THE TAIL**

**THE HEAD**

**THE BILL**

**THE LEGS**

**ANGLE OF THE WING**

## Wavelike Flight Path

**1 PROPULSION**

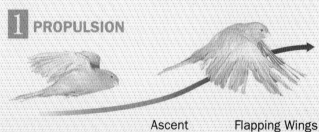

**2 REST**

Ascent     Flapping Wings     Folded-up Wings     Descent

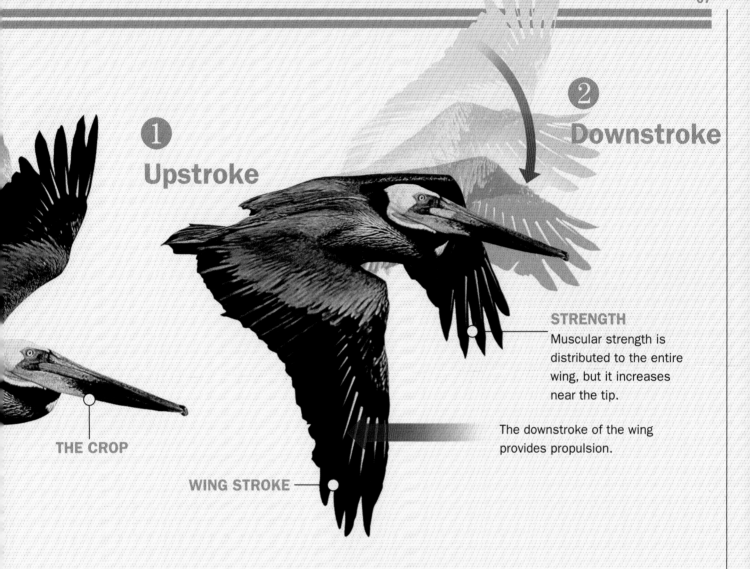

# ① Upstroke

# ② Downstroke

**STRENGTH**
Muscular strength is distributed to the entire wing, but it increases near the tip.

The downstroke of the wing provides propulsion.

**THE CROP**

**WING STROKE**

# Marine Birds

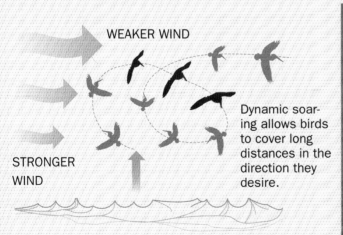

WEAKER WIND

STRONGER WIND

Dynamic soaring allows birds to cover long distances in the direction they desire.

3 to 33 feet (1-10 m) is the range in altitude for dynamic soaring.

# Landing

Flapping Against the Wind

Open Wings

Spread Tail

WIND

Sliding

The feet spread open before landing to provide more resistance and help the bird to slow down.

# Migration Routes

Cape Gannet

Rocky
Mountains

NORTH
AMERICA

EUROP

Snow Bunting

Peregrine
Falcon

*Mississippi River*

AMERICAN PACIFIC FLYWAY

**RUBY-THROATED
HUMMINGBIRD**

# 500 miles
## (800 km)

**IS THE DISTANCE THEY FLY
NONSTOP ACROSS THE
GULF OF MEXICO. THEY DO
IT IN JUST 20 HOURS.**

*Gulf of
Mexico*

ATLANTIC FLYWAY

CENTRAL
AMERICA

MISSISSIPPI FLYWAY

*Atlantic
Ocean*

*Amazon*

Barn Swallow

## Behavior

*Migratory* routes tend to be fixed, although
some migratory birds do not always follow
them exactly. The colors on the map indicate
the most important routes.

SOUTH
AMERICA

White Stork

American Golden Plover

## TYPES OF MIGRATION

Altitudinal

Latitudinal

Longitudinal

*Andes
Mountains*

**ARCTIC TERN**

# 25,000 miles
## (40,000 km)

**IS THE DISTANCE IT CAN COVER ON
ITS ROUND-TRIP MIGRATION BETWEEN
THE POLES. IT IS THE LONGEST
MIGRATION IN THE WORLD.**

*Antarctic Ocean*

ANTARCTIC FLYWAY

CENTRAL ASIA FLYWAY

Northern Wheatear

Bewick's Swan

*Ural Mountains*

*Altai Mountains*

*Caspian Sea*

Siberian Crane

*Sea of Japan*

BLACK SEA FLYWAY

*Himalayan Mountains*

Dead Sea

Barn Swallow

Greater Spotted Eagle

AFRICA

*Pacific Ocean*

MEETING POINT

# 1 billion

BIRDS MEET IN THE DEAD SEA VALLEY EVERY YEAR WHERE THE ASIAN, EUROPEAN, AND AFRICAN MIGRATION ROUTES CONVERGE.

Bar-headed Goose

*Kilimanjaro*

EASTERN ASIA FLYWAY

*Indian Ocean*

Curlew Sandpiper

## How They Find Their Way Around

Birds use a compass-and-triangulation system that lets them know where they are according to the position of the sun or stars.

OCEANIA

Azimuthal Angle: Sun/Trajectory

**South**

Southwest

EASTERN ASIA FLYWAY

**West**

Flight Direction: Northeast to Southwest

Caspian Tern

Northeast

**North**

Wandering Albatross

# Nuptial Parade

Finding a mate is not easy for any species. For birds, the exhibition of plumage with bright colors, the presentation of offerings and gifts, and the performance of dances and highly elaborate flight patterns are some of the particular behaviors seen during this period. They are known as nuptial or courtship displays. The male resorts to all these strategic gestures to attract the female's attention and prevent her from paying attention to other males. Some of these rituals are extremely complicated; others are very tender and delicate.

**DISPLAYING PHYSICAL ATTRIBUTES**

**BUILDING BOWERS**

**GIFTS**

## Incubation

Some birds have a brood patch, which helps keep the egg warm.

BROOD PATCH

# 5.9 feet (1.8 m)

**IS THE SIZE OF THE TAIL OF THE PEACOCK WHEN IT
UNFURLS ITS MORE THAN 200 SHINING FEATHERS
AND FORMS A FAN TO ATTRACT THE FEMALE.**

**Gray Crowned
Crane**

**Emperor
Penguin**

# Incubation Duration
by Species

| PIGEON | PENGUIN | ALBATROSS |
|---|---|---|
| 18 days | 62 days | 80 days |

# Where They Live

Most birds have specific habitats determined by climate and geographic features. Count de Buffon in the 18th century was the first person to notice that living beings are not distributed homogeneously. By analyzing how animals were dispersed on the planet, he realized that different places had different types of fauna. After the work of naturalist Charles Darwin and ornithologist Philip Sclater, it became clear that *organisms* are situated in specific biogeographic regions.

**Puffin** ▲

NORTH AMERICA

## Nearctic

**7%**

## 732 Species
62 families

### CHARACTERISTICS

Climatic barrier of cold weather and oceanic isolation

Most migrating species

Many *insectivorous* and aquatic birds

Affinity with Palearctic

Kinds of Birds: **loons and puffins**

*Pacific Ocean*

## Oceania

**2%**

## 187 Species
15 families

### CHARACTERISTICS

Large area and number of climates

Gliders, divers, and swimmers

Abundance of fish-eating species

Many cosmopolitan species

Kinds of Birds: **albatrosses, sheathbills, petrels, penguins, and seagulls**

## Adaptations According to the Environment

Birds have undergone a highly varied array of changes in form and behavior.

SOUTH AMERICA

*Atlantic Ocean*

## Neotropic

**32%**

## 3,370 Species
86 families

### CHARACTERISTICS

Long-lasting geographic isolation

Many primitive species

Great numbers of frugivores

Kinds of Birds: **rheas, tinamous, oilbirds, hoatzins, cotingas, and stripe-backed antbirds**

◄ **Hoatzin**

# Biodiversity in the World

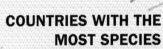

**NUMBER OF SPECIES**

- up to 200
- 200 - 400
- 400 - 600
- 600 - 800
- 800 - 1,000
- 1,000 - 1,200
- 1,200 - 1,400
- 1,400 - 1,600
- 1,600 - 1,800

## COUNTRIES WITH THE MOST SPECIES

**More than 1,500**
Colombia
Brazil
Peru
Ecuador
Indonesia

**More than 1,000**
Bolivia
Venezuela
China
India
Mexico
Democratic Republic of the Congo
Tanzania
Kenya
Argentina

ASIA
EUROPE
AFRICA
*Indian Ocean*
*Pacific Ocean*
OCEANIA

## Palearctic

**937** **Species**
73 families

9%

### CHARACTERISTICS
Climatic barrier of cold weather and oceanic isolation

Low diversity of species

Most are migratory species

Many insectivorous and aquatic birds

Kinds of Birds: **wood grouse, waxwings, flycatchers, cranes**

## Afrotropic

**1,950** **Species**
73 families

19%

### CHARACTERISTICS
Maritime and desert isolation

Great number of Passeriformes

Many flightless birds

Kinds of Birds: **ostriches, turacos, cuckoos**

## Indomalaya

**1,700** **Species**
66 families

16%

### CHARACTERISTICS
Affinities with the Afrotropical zone

Tropical birds

Many frugivores

Kinds of Birds: **ioras, pittas, swifts**

## Australasia

**1,590** **Species**
64 families

15%

### CHARACTERISTICS
Long isolation

Many flightless and primitive birds

Kinds of Birds: **emus, kiwis, cockatoos, birds of paradise**

▲ **Ruby-Throated Hummingbird**

◀ **Ostrich**

# Talkative and Colorful

Parrots form a very attractive bird group with a great capacity for learning. This group comprises cockatoos, macaws, and parakeets. They share physical characteristics, such as a big head, a short neck, a strong hook-shaped *bill*, and climbing feet. They have plumage in many colors. Toucans and woodpeckers share with parrots the colors of their *feathers* and their type of feet.

THE BILL OF AN IBIS

THE LEGS OF AN IBIS

White Ibis

Woodpeckers hollow out tree trunks with pecks in order to build a nest and to feed on insects that eat wood.

THE HABITAT OF WOODPECKERS

◄ Toucans

Quetzals ►

COMPARISON

COMPARISON   0 in or cm

**MONK PARAKEET**
Argentina
12–14 in (30–35 cm)

20 in (50 cm)   **COCKATOO**
Mexico
16–20 in
(40–50 cm)

**HYACINTH MACAW**
Brazil/Bolivia
39 in (100 cm)

39 in (100 cm)

WINGS

The F

FEET LIKE HANDS

FEATHERS AND COLORS

NOSTRILS

# Eating, Climbing
# and Chattering

Parrots use their excellent memory
to imitate sounds.

**HOOKED BILL**

# Armed to Hunt

Birds of prey are perfectly equipped to eat living animals. Their eyesight is three times sharper than that of human beings, their ears are designed to determine the precise status of their prey, they have strong, sharp talons, and they can kill a small mammal with the pressure of their talons alone. Their hook-shaped      can kill prey by tearing its neck with a single peck.

## Diurnal and Nocturnal

Eurasian Eagle Owl

Bald Eagle

# 5 miles
## (8 km)
**IS THE DISTANCE FROM WHICH A FALCON CAN PERCEIVE A PIGEON.**

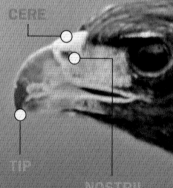

CERE

TIP

NOSTRIL

▲ **Zone-tailed Hawk**

## Bills

BALD EAGLE

SPARROW HAWK

FALCON

GOSHAWK

OWL PELLETS

HOW THE
VULTURE HUNTS

DIMENSIONS

GLIDING
ABILITY

Condors 3 to 9.5 ft (0.95-2.9 m)

Eagles 4.5 to 8 ft (1.35–2.45 m)

Buzzards
4 to 5 ft (1.2–1.5 m)

FINDING
FOOD

Kites 2.6 to 6.4 ft (0.8–1.95 m)

Red-Backed Hawk
3.4 to 4.4 ft (1.05–1.35 m)

Falcons
2.2 to 4.1 ft (0.67–1.25 m)

Feet

GRIFFON
VULTURE

FISHING EAGLE

GOSHAWK

SPARROW
HAWK

# The Perchers Club

Passerines form the widest and most diverse order of birds. What distinguishes them? Their feet are suited for perching and, therefore, for living among trees, although they can also stroll on the ground and through the brush. They inhabit terrestrial environments all over the world, from deserts to groves. Their complex sounds and songs originate from a very well-developed syrinx. In their youth, they are agile and vivacious, with very attractive, abundant, and colorful plumage.

**PASSERIFORMES BIRDS**

## 50%

**THE PERCENTAGE OF BIRDS THAT ARE INCLUDED IN THE ORDER PASSERIFORMES**

**THE SMALLEST**

**HUMMINGBIRDS**
2 IN (5 CM)

**SWALLOWS**
7 IN (19 CM)

**RAVENS**
26 IN (65 CM)

## Family Album
These birds are all passerines.

**LYREBIRDS**

HARD, SHORT
BILL

**Blue-and-white**
**Swallow** ▶

SYRINX

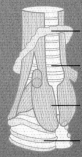

Syringeal
Cartilage

Tracheal Ring

Bronchial
Muscles

Bronchial Ring

LIVING AT THE
EXTREMES

A

B

PERCHING
POST

(A) SUMMER

(B) WINTER

BARN SWALLOW

WIDE BILLS

OVENBIRDS AND
THEIR RELATIVES

# Endangered Species

The cutting of trees in rainforests and woodlands has destroyed many bird habitats, the loss of which is the leading cause of bird extinctions today. Also, the introduction of animals such as cats, dogs, and rats to new areas has created a threat for many bird species. Indirect poisoning with pesticides, the trafficking of exotic birds as pets, and the sale of feathers have done further damage to many species. Fortunately, all is not lost. The first step to conserving the world's birds is to learn about the extinction of birds and its magnitude.

HYACINTH MACAW

CALIFORNIA CONDOR

## The Most Important Causes

Hunting, human encroachment, the introduction of foreign species, and pollution all contribute to extinction.

POISONING

**1** PESTICIDES

Granivorous Birds

**2** ACCUMULATED POISON

Birds of Prey

**3** INCREASING LEVELS

PEREGRINE FALCON

YELLOW-CRESTED COCKATOO

INDIAN VULTURE